THERE WAS A BIRD

Franicia White

There Was a Bird

by *Franicia Tomokane White*

A WHOLESOME PRESS SOFTCOVER
Copyright © 2016 by Franicia Tomokane White

Wholesome Press
PMB # 24639 PO Box 2428, Pensacola, FL 32513
Website: Wholesome.Press

ISBN: 978-1-943449-21-7
Printed in the United States of America

Illustrations and Book Design by Franicia White
Photography by Timothy White
www.timandfranicia.com

This book is a gift for:

_____

_____

_____

To Tim and our sweet children:
I love you all dearly and am
so thankful to the Lord
for you!

Dear Reader,
I have enjoyed creating this book for you!
May it be a great blessing.
❀ Franicia T. White

There was a

BIRD

BIRD

BIRD.

Who needed a

HOME
HOME
HOME.

" I'll build a
place, place, place

To call my

own, own, own."

She got some

STICKS
STICKS
STICKS

And built

ALONG
ALONG
ALONG.

She made it

cozy cozy cozy

And made it

STRONG
STRONG
STRONG.

Up on a

tree, tree, tree

There sat the

nest, nest, nest.

And it was

time, time, time

For its

test, test, test.

The rain came

DOWN

DOWN

DOWN!

The winds did

BLOW

BLOW

BLOW.

The nest was **strong, strong, strong.**

It would not **go, go, go!**

Then it was

time, time, time.

The bird did

stay, stay, stay.

The bird was glad, glad, glad.
It sang a song, song, song.

Oh happy **day, day, day!**

The bird's a **mom, mom, mom!**

www.ingramcontent.com/pod-product-compliance
Lightning Source LLC
Chambersburg PA
CBHW050800110526
44588CB00003B/63